Artistic Scroll Saw Patterns & Projects

Artistic Scroll Saw
Patterns & Projects

Patrick Spielman & Dan Kihl

Sterling Publishing Co., Inc.
New York

The written instructions, photographs, designs, patterns, and projects in this volume are intended for the personal use of the reader and may be reproduced for that purpose only. Any other use, especially commercial use, is forbidden under law without the written permission of the copyright holder.

Every effort has been made to ensure that all the information in this book is accurate. However, due to differing conditions, tools, and individual skills, the publisher cannot be responsible for any injuries, losses, and other damages that may result from the use of the information in this book.

Library of Congress Cataloging-in-Publication Data

Spielman, Patrick E.
    Artistic scroll saw patterns & projects / Patrick Spielman & Dan Kihl.
        p.   cm.
    Includes index.
    ISBN 0-8069-9424-X
    1. Jig saws.   2. Woodwork—Patterns.   I. Kihl, Dan.   II. Title.
TT186.S6636   1997
745.51'3—dc21   97-31775
                                                                CIP

10 9 8 7 6 5 4 3 2 1

Published by Sterling Publishing Company, Inc.
387 Park Avenue South, New York, N.Y. 10016
© 1997 by Patrick Spielman and Dan Kihl
Distributed in Canada by Sterling Publishing
% Canadian Manda Group, One Atlantic Avenue, Suite 105
Toronto, Ontario, Canada M6K 3E7
Distributed in Great Britain and Europe by Cassell PLC
Wellington House, 125 Strand, London WC2R 0BB, England
Distributed in Australia by Capricorn Link (Australia) Pty Ltd.
P.O. Box 6651, Baulkham Hills, Business Centre, NSW 2153, Australia
Printed and Bound in Hong Kong
All rights reserved

Sterling ISBN 0-8069-9424-X

CONTENTS

COLOR SECTION FOLLOWS PAGE 32

INTRODUCTION

This book offers a variety of new, unusual, and artistic designs and patterns for the scrolling enthusiast. Included are a number of color photographs that illustrate the projects and hopefully will stimulate the reader to consider using a variety of materials and finishes. Readers are also encouraged to use the patterns in enlarged or reduced versions for various applications. Imagine some designs greatly enlarged as pieces of yard art or as large wall decorations in home or business settings. Many of the patterns in reduced versions make eye-catching jewelry, great appliqués with clocks, signs, furniture decorations, and look good on household accessories such as jewelry and tissue boxes.

We have not included basic woodworking instructions for applying and using the patterns. This, we feel, would be a repeat of information provided in our earlier successful book *Southwest Scroll Saw Patterns*. This information is also readily available in many other books and is, by and large, common knowledge among today's scrollers. We have, therefore, dedicated that space to more patterns, which we feel will be of greater interest and benefit to our readers.

We sincerely hope these patterns will be appreciated and thoroughly enjoyed by all artists who work and fashion items with the scroll saw for ornamental and decorative purposes.

Patrick Spielman and Dan Kihl
January 1997

FLOWERS

Iris.

Iris.

Flowers.

Dragonfly with flowers.

BIRDS

Pelicans.

Seagulls.

Parrot.

Hummingbird.

Eight birds.

*Hummingbirds. Insert contrasting inlays
into the open areas of the birds and flowers.*

16

SEA AND WATER LIFE

Shark and diver.

Whales.

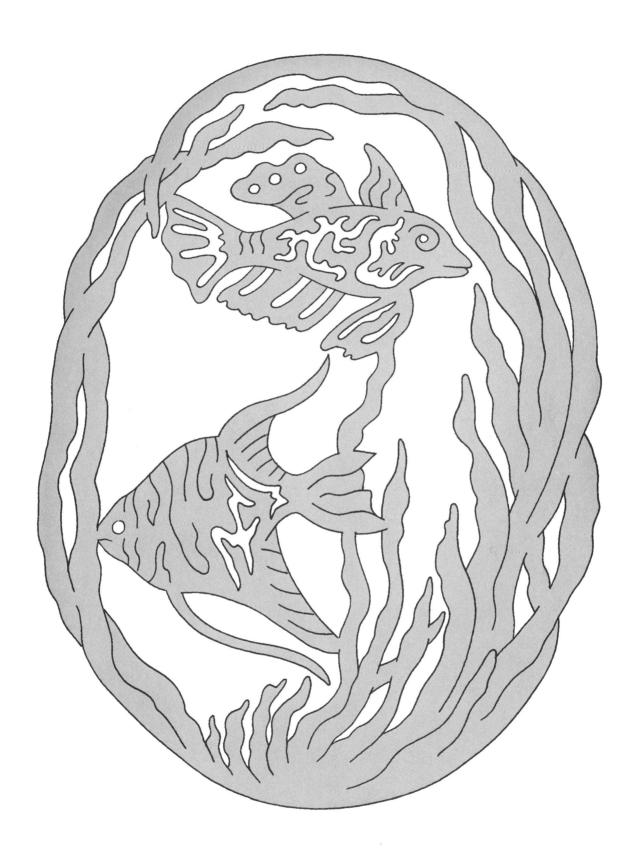

Tropical fish.

Dolphins

Dolphins, in a Southwest design.

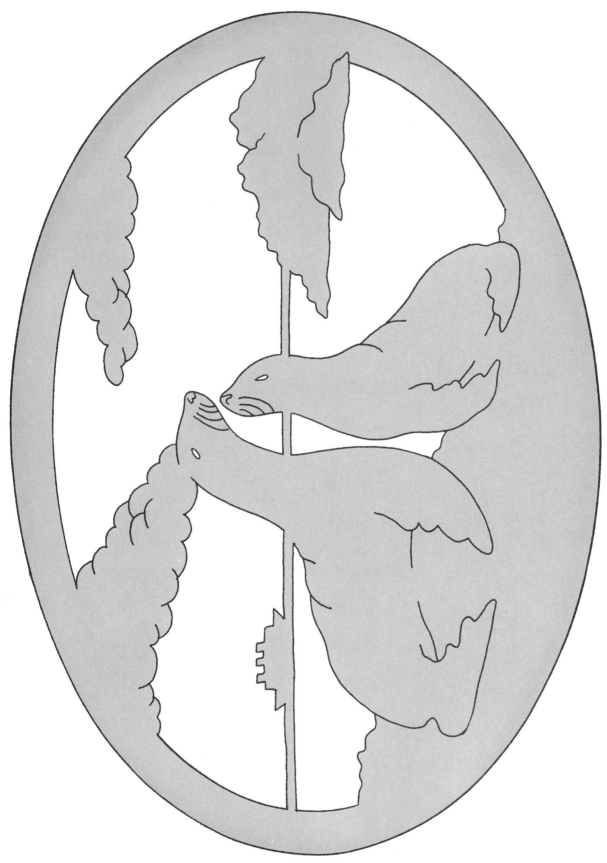

Seals.

Koi.

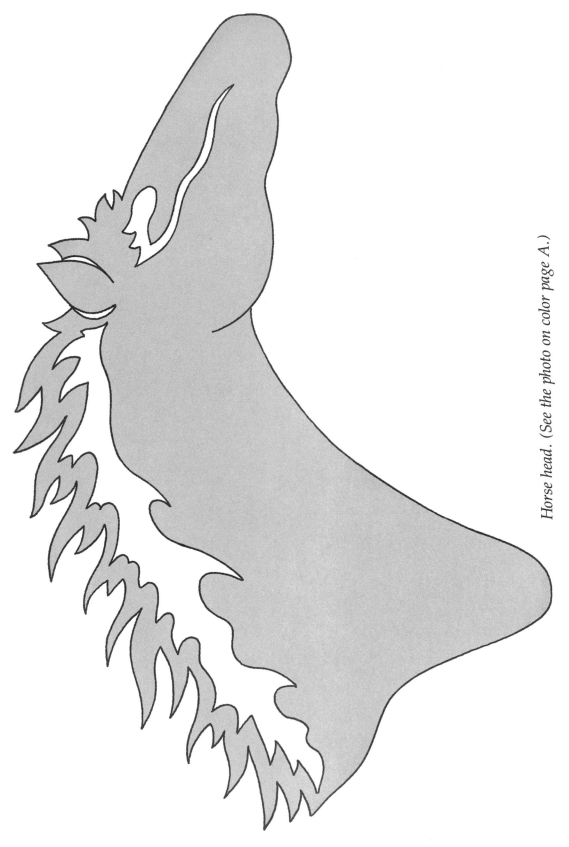

Horse head. (See the photo on color page A.)

Wild horses. (See the photo on color page A.)

25

Wild horses.

Wild horses.

Horses and dust cloud.

Horse and dust cloud.

Horses.

Horse.

Carousel horse.

Horse heads cut from ¼-inch-thick padauk (above) and ¼-inch-thick mahogany, and with oil finishes. The pattern is on page 24.

Wild horses of ¼-inch-thick stained birch plywood on a painted background. The patterns are on pages 25–27.

Elephants in tusk cut from unfinished ¼-inch-thick birch plywood. The pattern is on page 33.

Gazelle cut from ¼-inch-thick unfinished birch plywood. The base is made of natural mahogany, and has a 15-degree bevel-sawn edge. (Photo reprinted from Patrick Spielman's *Home Workshop News*.) The patterns are on pages 34 and 35.

A

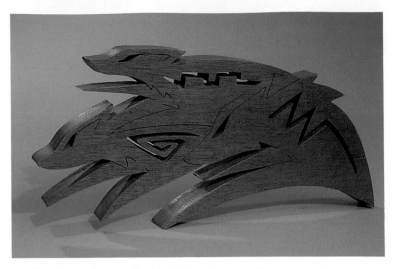

Wolf pack cut from ¾-inch-thick mahogany. The pattern is on page 48.

Deer and wolf cut from ¼-inch-unfinished birch plywood. They are set off on a ¾-inch-thick mahogany plaque with ¼-inch spacers. The pattern is on page 50.

Giraffes cut out of thin, unfinished birch plywood. (Photo reprinted from Patrick Spielman's *Home Workshop News.*) The pattern is on page 56.

Segmented deer cut from ¼-inch-thick birch plywood, stained and unfinished. The base is made of ¼-inch-thick solid mahogany, and has a 15-degree-bevel edge. The patterns are on pages 52 and 53.

This spider web cut out of thin plywood makes an unusual corner decoration. This is a good project for stack-cutting large quantities of material all at once. The pattern is on page 60.

"Three Amigos" cut from ¾-inch-thick walnut, and oil-finished. The pattern is on page 65.

Woman's heads in ¼-inch-thick clear acrylic plastic (left) and ¼-inch-thick tinted polycarbonate plastic (right). The pattern is on page 76.

"Coming of Age" cut from ¹⁄₁₆-inch or thinner unfinished birch, and overlaid on metallic painted backer. The pattern is on page 77.

C

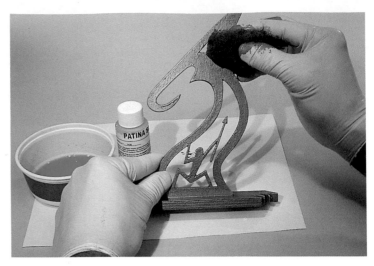

Using a sponge to apply the patina solution over a previously applied coat of liquid copper finish. This finish system by Modern Options and other manufacturers is easy to use and available in most craft and hobby stores.

Goat with hunter made of ⅜-inch-thick birch plywood, with a faux-patina metallic finish. The pattern is on page 79.

"Couple" made from ¼-inch-thick natural birch (left), and ¼-inch-thick painted birch (right). The pattern is on page 80.

"I'm So Confused" stack-cut from three different-colored materials ranging from ⅛ to ¼ inch thick. Here oak, stained basswood, and unfinished basswood are the materials used. The pattern is on page 82.

D

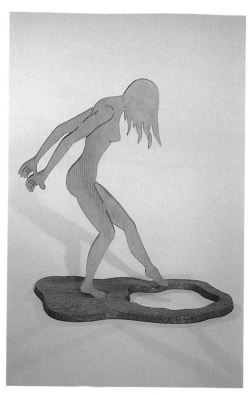

Woman with flowing hair cut from 1/16-inch-thick birch plywood overlaid on mahogany.
The pattern is on page 90.

Woman stepping in pond. The woman is cut from 1/4-inch-thick birch plywood. The 1/4-inch-thick mahogany base has 15-degree-bevel edges. Blue paper glued to the base represents water. The patterns are on pages 88 and 89.

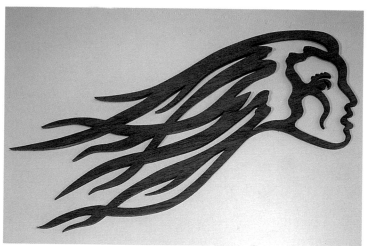

Man's head cut from thin, solid mahogany. The pattern is on page 97.

Woman's head with feathers made of 1/16-inch-thick birch plywood overlaid on simulated granite. The pattern is on page 93.

E

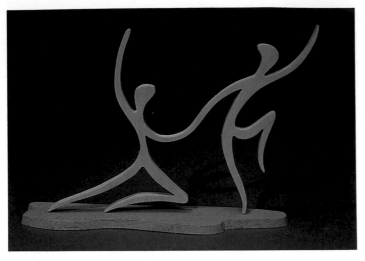

Dancers cut from ¼-inch-thick unfinished birch plywood on a ¼-inch-thick mahogany base with a 15-degree-bevel edge. The patterns are on pages 104 and 105.

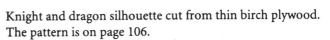

This dragon table is made from ¼-inch-thick Baltic birch plywood. It has a black-painted bottom assembly, and a patina-finished top. The patterns are on pages 108–110.

Knight and dragon silhouette cut from thin birch plywood. The pattern is on page 106.

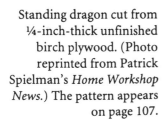

Standing dragon cut from ¼-inch-thick unfinished birch plywood. (Photo reprinted from Patrick Spielman's *Home Workshop News*.) The pattern appears on page 107.

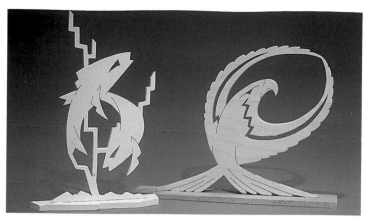

At left are southwest fish made of painted plywood. At right is an eagle made of natural birch plywood. The patterns are found on pages 21 and 112.

Eagle with feathers made from 1/16-inch-thick plywood overlaid on simulate granite. The pattern is on page 115.

Man in feather cut from 1/4-inch-thick solid mahogany. The pattern is on page 117.

Kokopelli in ring with feathers, which is cut from a copper sheet and has a patina finish. Note the twist on the feather's quills. For this pattern and alternate designs, see page 125.

G

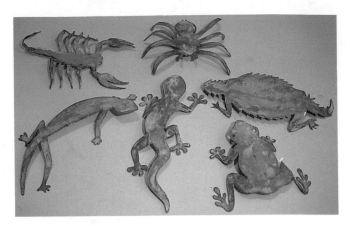

Various critters made from bent metal (copper), with green and blue patina finishes. For patterns, turn to pages 130 and 132–135.

Close-up views of a bent-metal frog, lizard, and gecko, with a patina solution on the right.

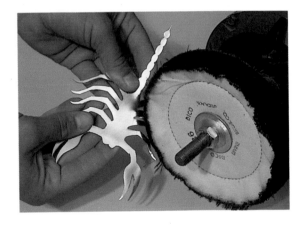

After sawing the bent-metal critter, remove sharp burr edges with a buffing wheel charged with tripoli or other buffing compound. Note: Apply lacquer or a clear vinyl finish to the polished copper. To apply a patina finish, the surfaces must be roughened with 180–150 grit abrasive prior to the application of the patina solution.

A copper critter with a patina finish (above), and one with a polished surface that has a lacquer finish (below).

H

MISCELLANEOUS ANIMALS

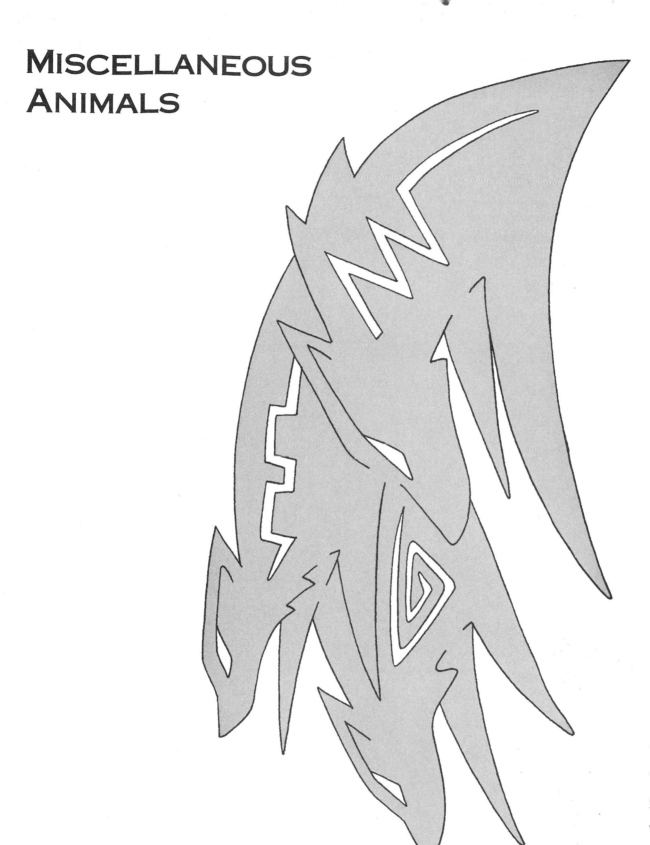

Wolf pack. (See the photo on page B of the color section.)

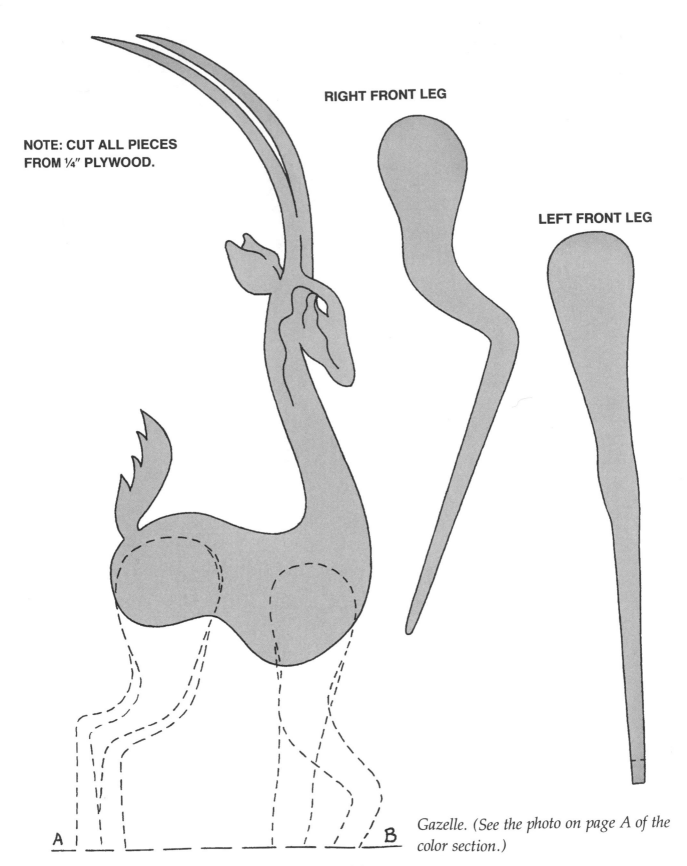

NOTE: CUT ALL PIECES FROM ¼" PLYWOOD.

RIGHT FRONT LEG

LEFT FRONT LEG

A

B

Gazelle. (See the photo on page A of the color section.)

34

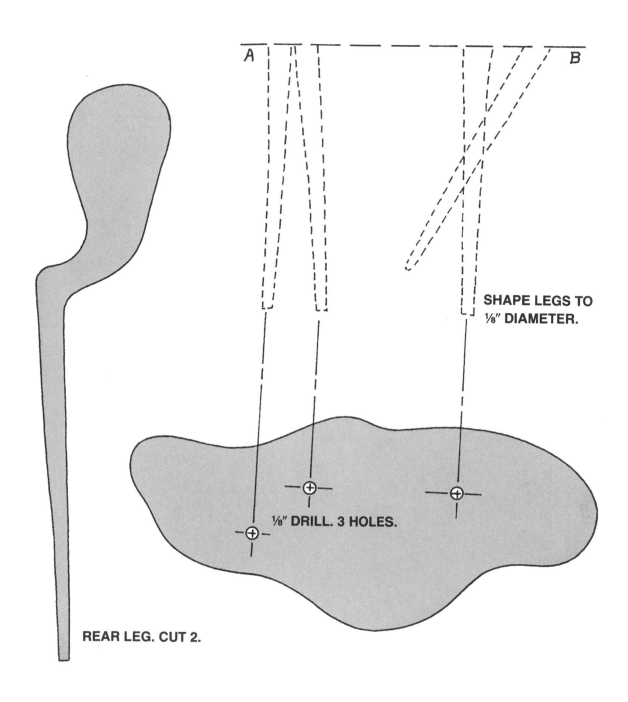

A   B

SHAPE LEGS TO ⅛″ DIAMETER.

⅛″ DRILL. 3 HOLES.

REAR LEG. CUT 2.

Rear leg and base for gazelle on previous page.

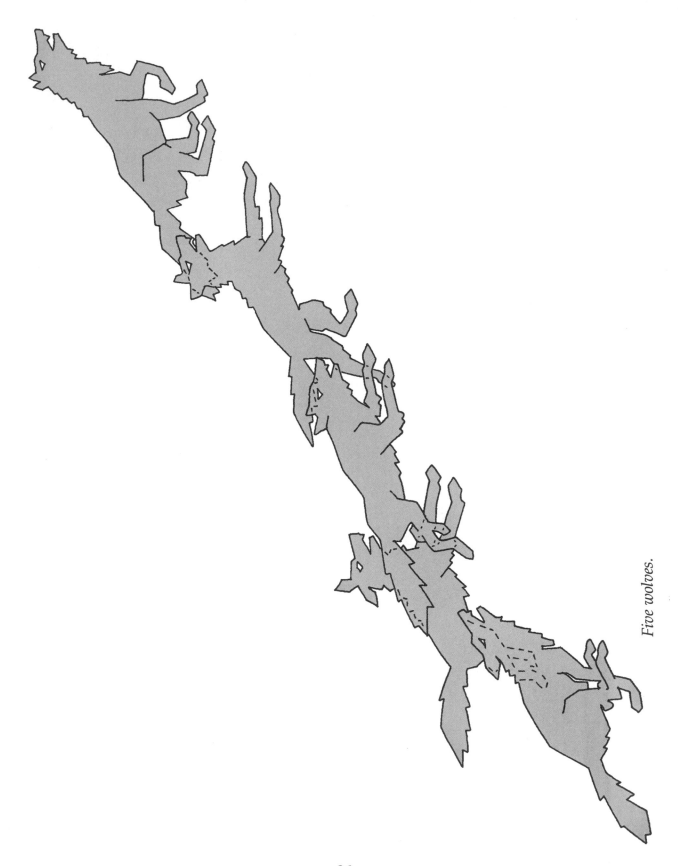

Five wolves.

Patterns for five wolves.

Patterns for five wolves.

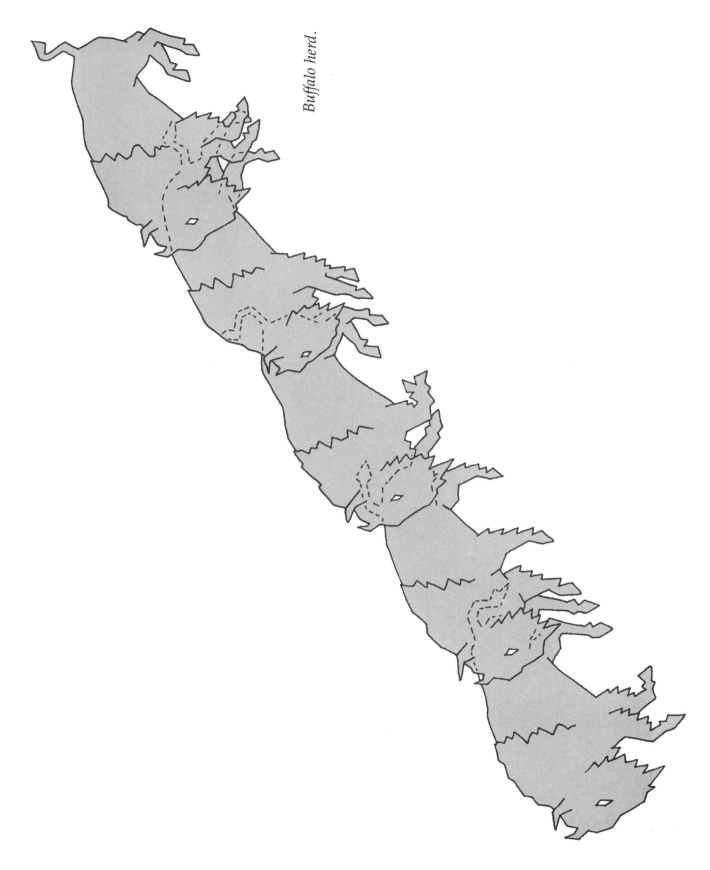

Buffalo herd.

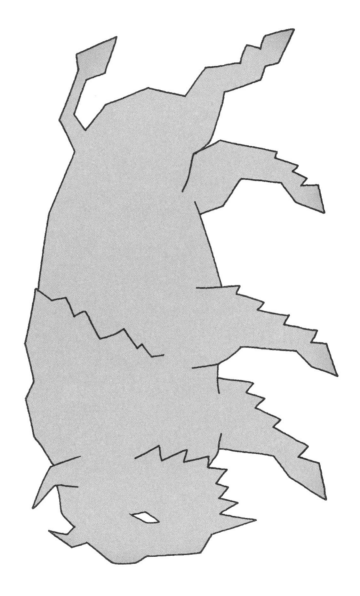

Buffalo pattern.

Buffalo patterns.

Buffalo patterns.

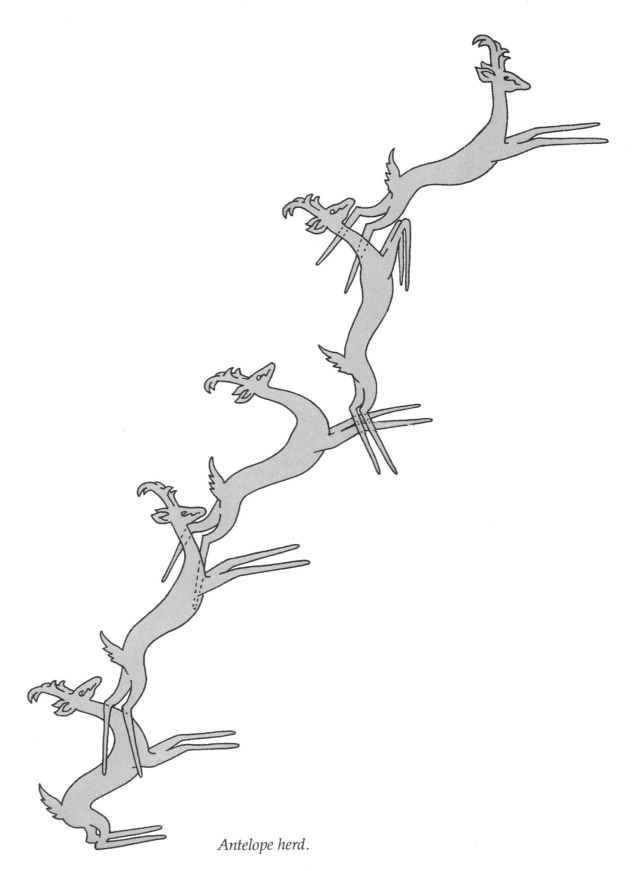

Antelope herd.

Antelope patterns.

44

Antelope pattern.

Antelope pattern.

Antelope pattern.

47

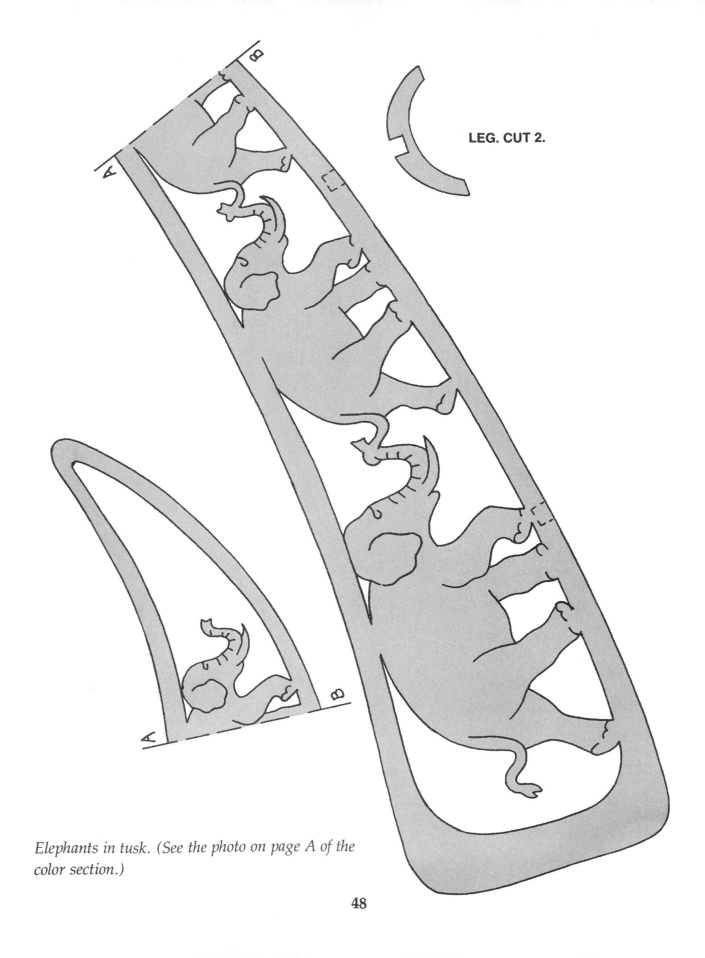

LEG. CUT 2.

Elephants in tusk. (See the photo on page A of the color section.)

48

Charging goat.

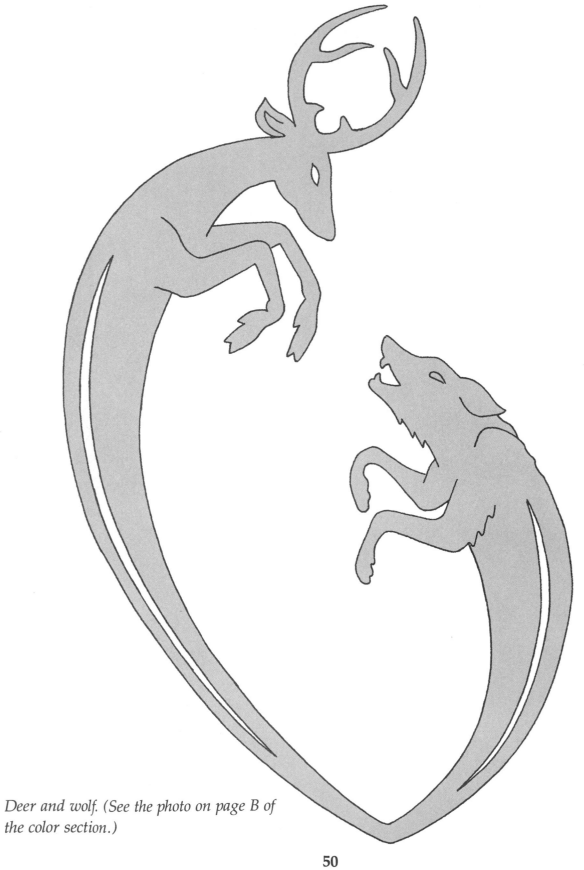

Deer and wolf. (See the photo on page B of the color section.)

Bears and squirrel.

Jumping deer. (See the photo on page B of the color section.)

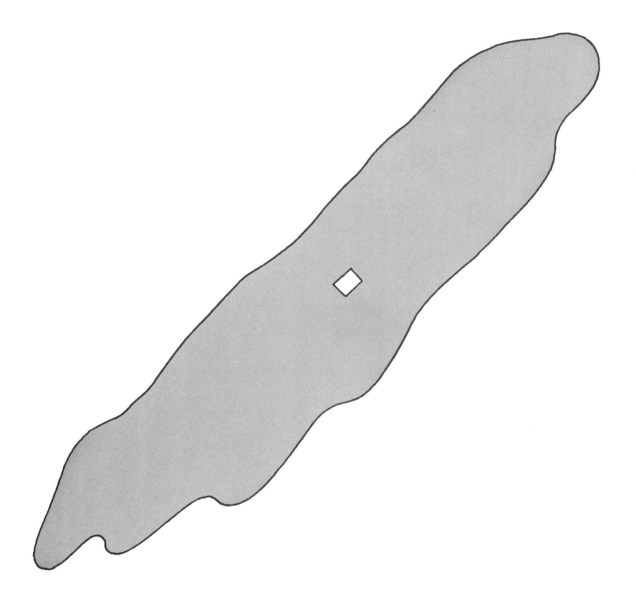

Jumping deer base.

Moose.

54

Goat.

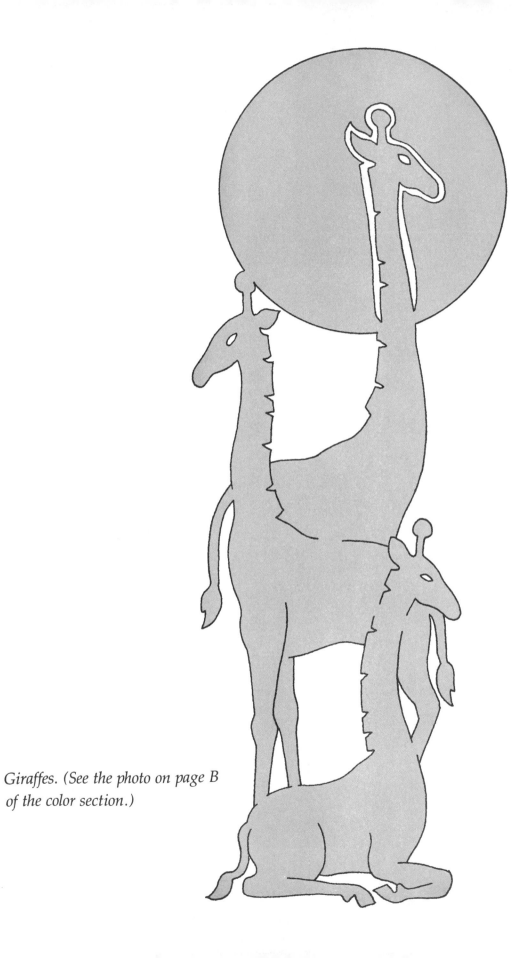

Giraffes. (See the photo on page B of the color section.)

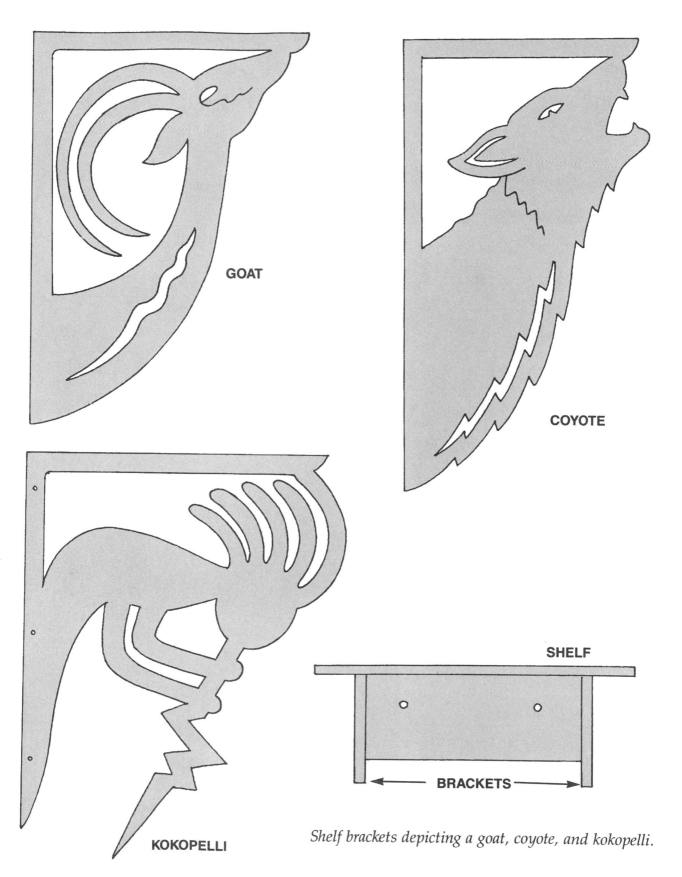

GOAT

COYOTE

SHELF

BRACKETS

KOKOPELLI

Shelf brackets depicting a goat, coyote, and kokopelli.

57

Coyote with moon and stars.

Buffalo skull.

MISCELLANEOUS FUN DESIGNS

Spider web. (See the photo on page C of the color section.)

Snake head.

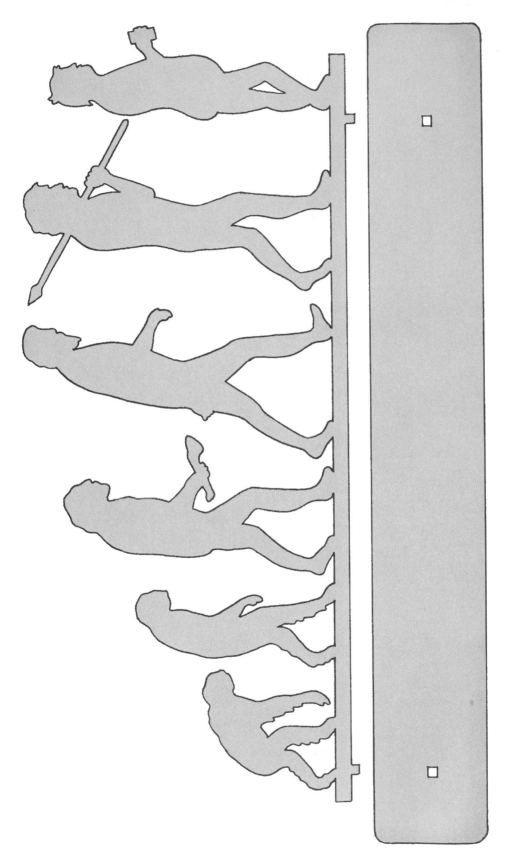

Evolution of Man.

"I was here the last time I was lost."

*First love. (Adapt any suitable
base design in the book to fit.)*

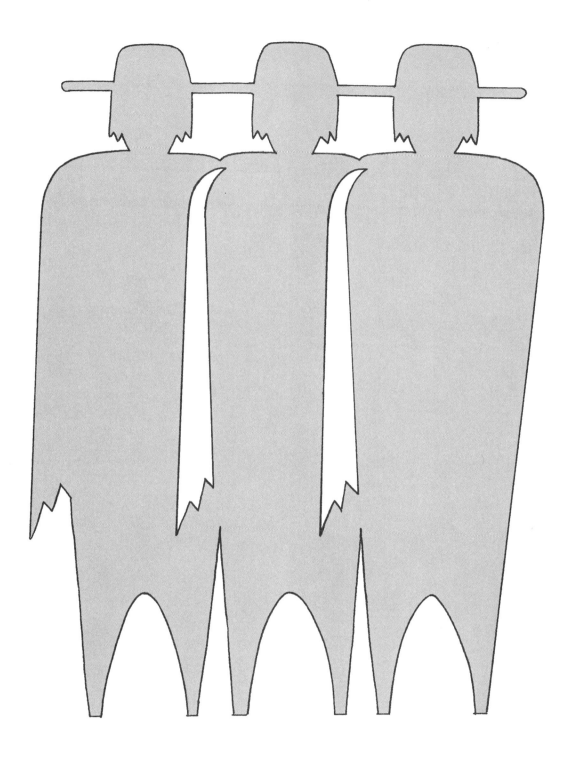

Three amigos. (See the photo on page C of the color section.)

PASTIMES

Bike race.

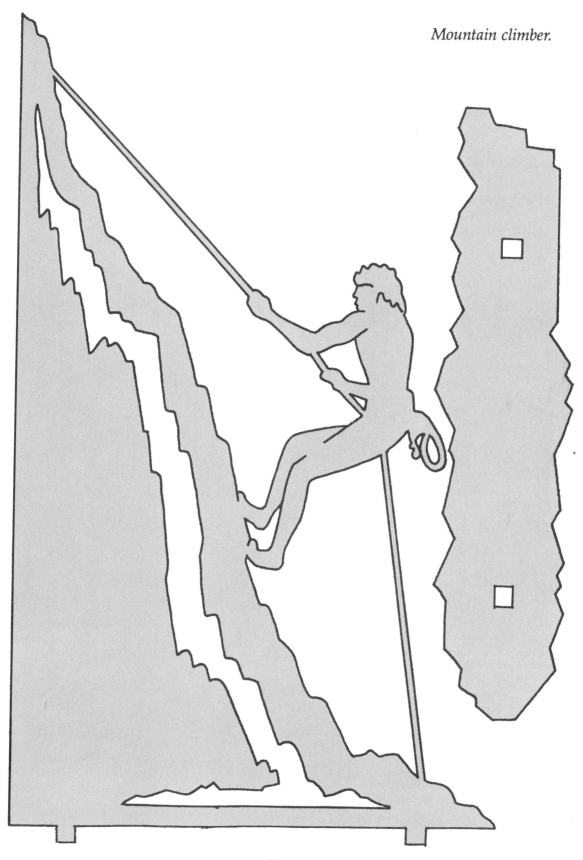

Mountain climber.

Fisherman.

Winter dream.

69

Summertime.

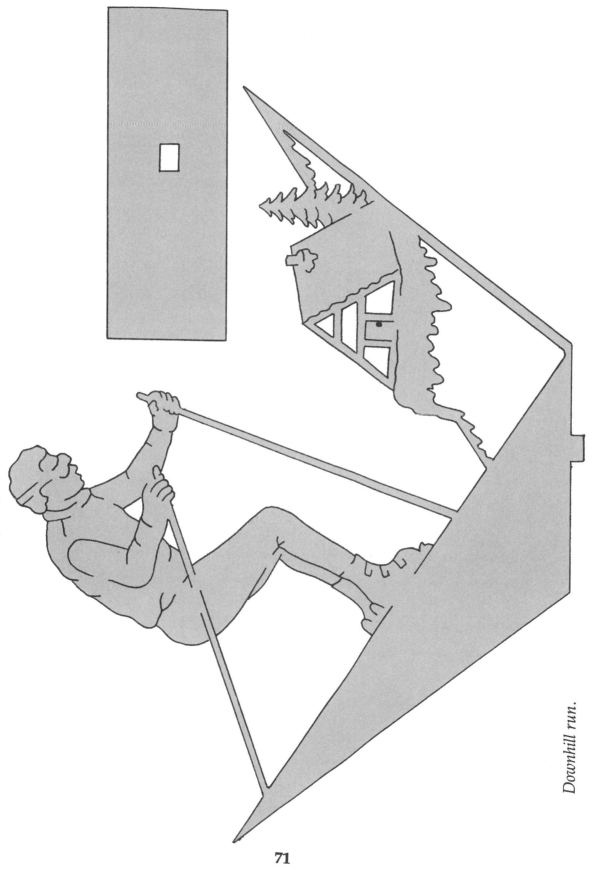

Downhill run.

Artist.

72

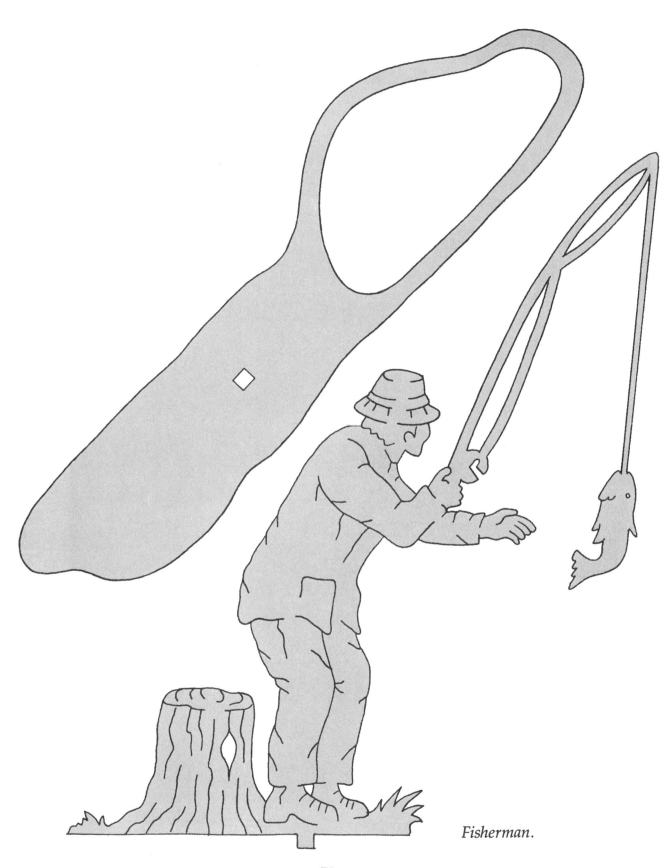

Fisherman.

WALL AND STANDING SCULPTURES

Bat.

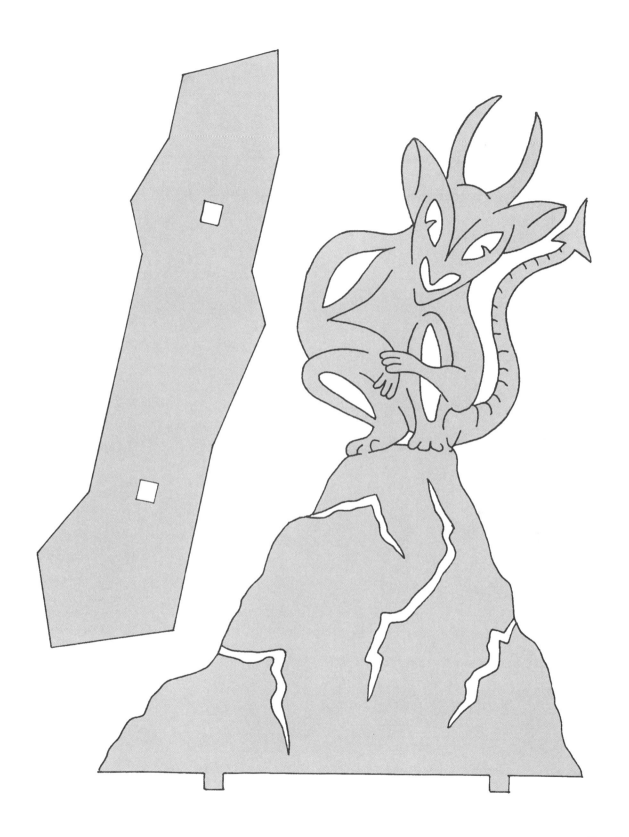

Devil.

Woman's head. (See photo on page C of the color section.)

Coming of age. (See photo on page C of the color section.)

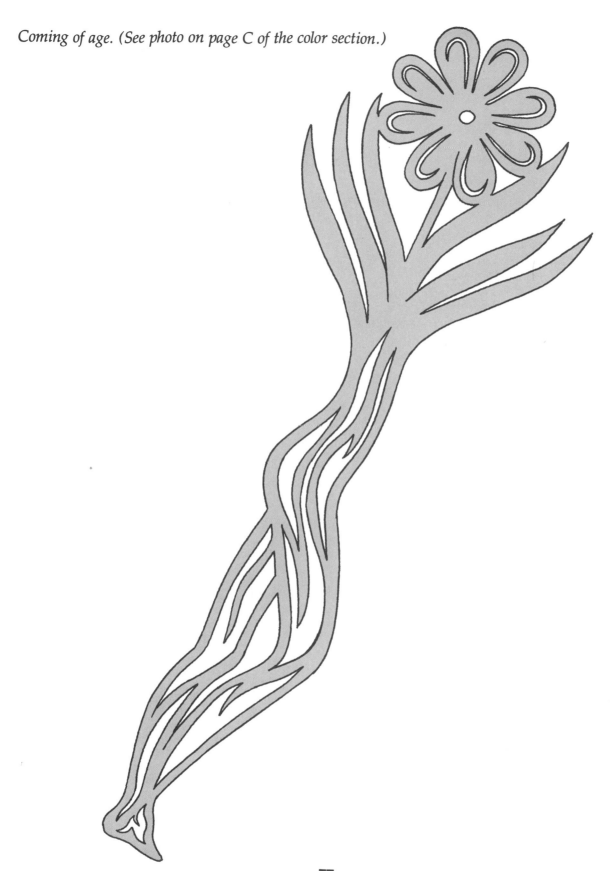

Morning stretch. (A contrasting inlay can be added to the space.)

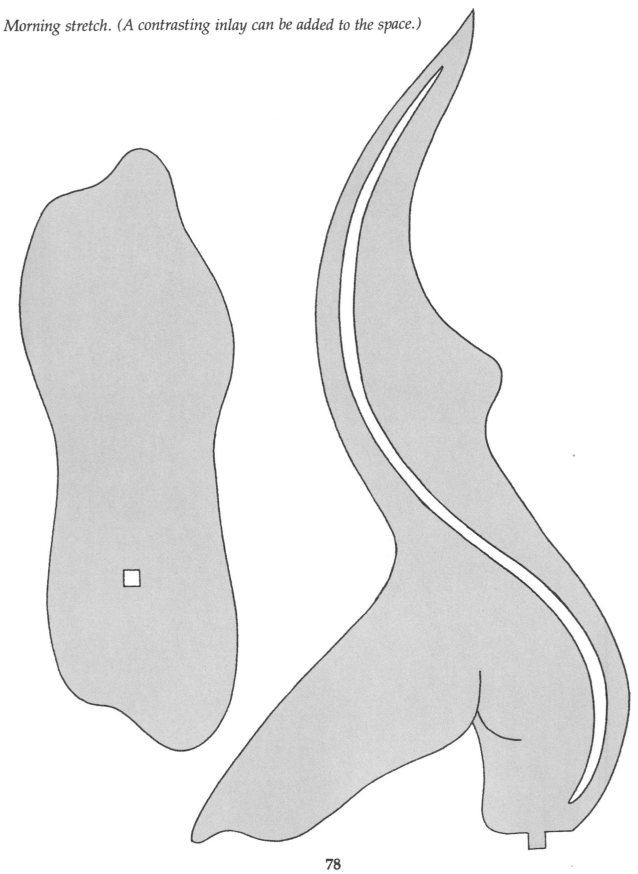

Goat with hunter. (See the photo on page D of the color section.)

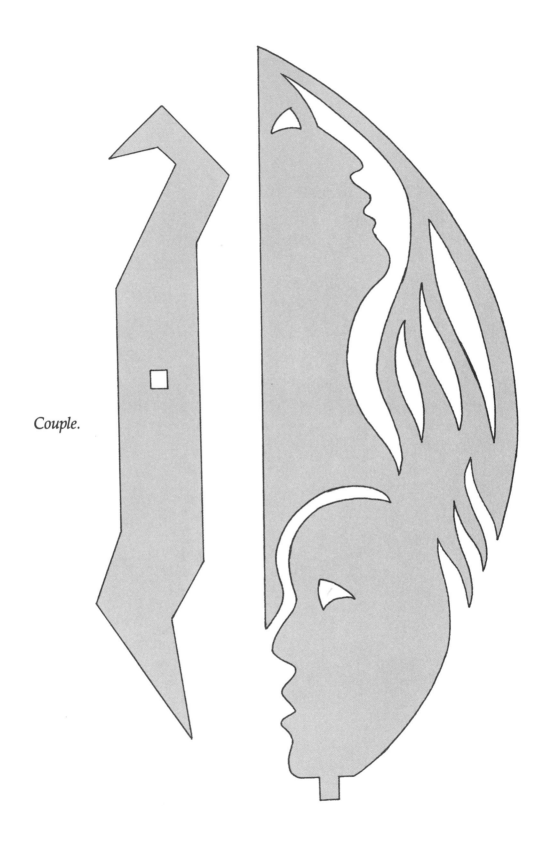

Couple.

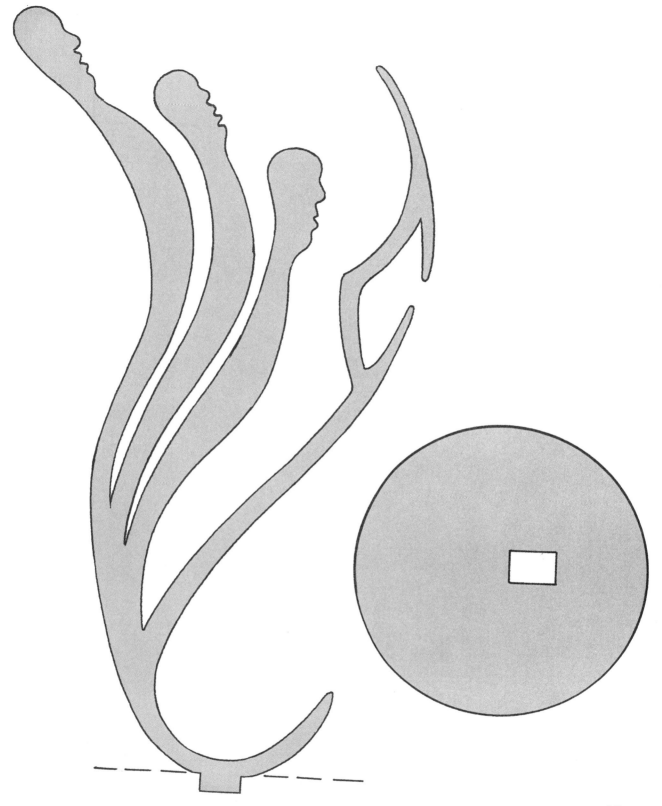

Vixen.

81

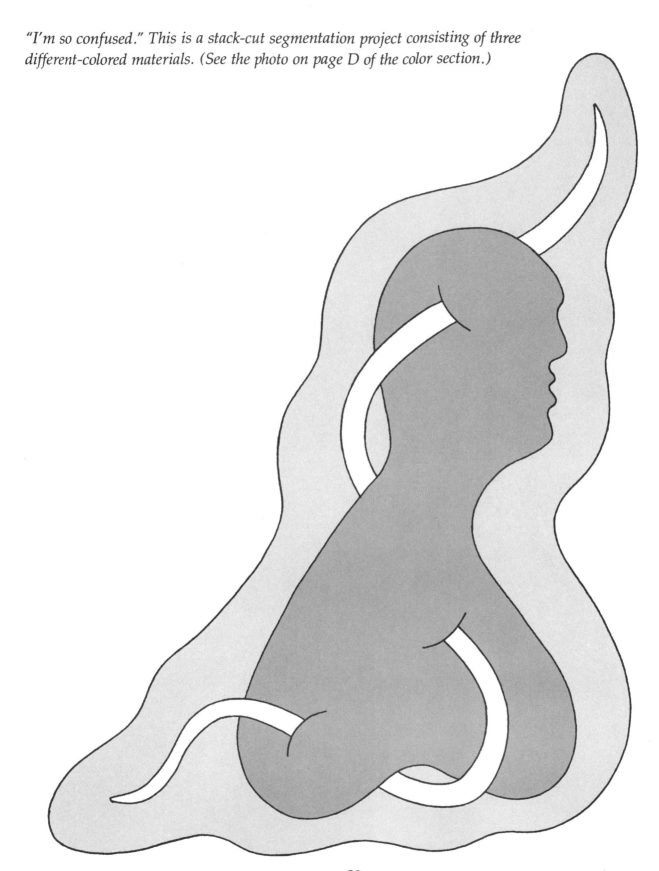

"I'm so confused." This is a stack-cut segmentation project consisting of three different-colored materials. (See the photo on page D of the color section.)

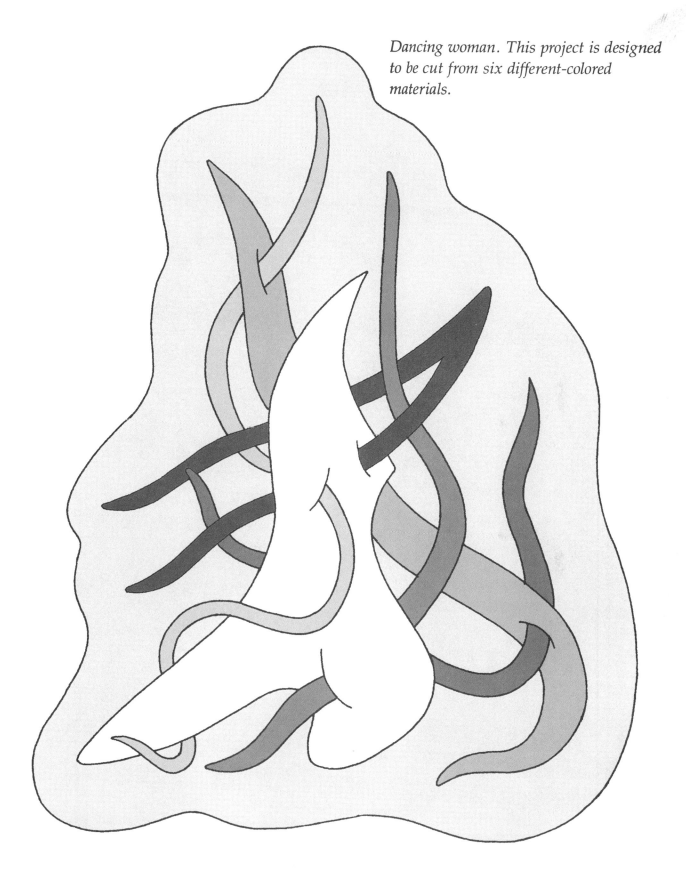

Dancing woman. This project is designed to be cut from six different-colored materials.

83

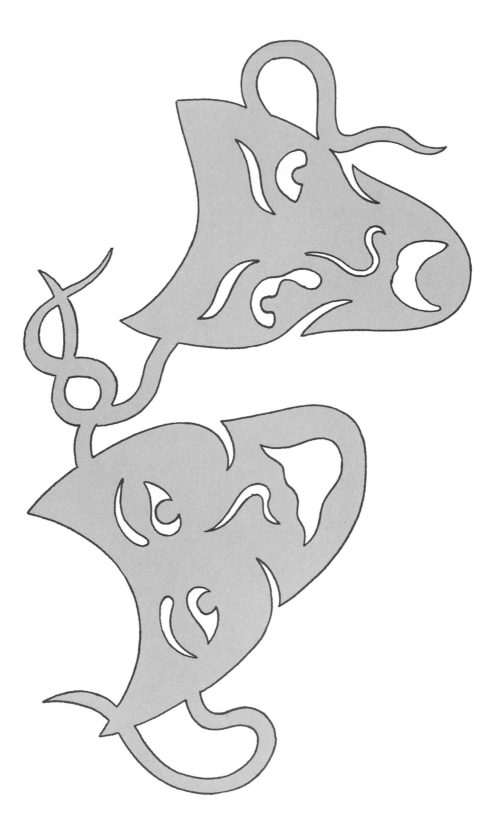

FEMALE FORMS

Girl.

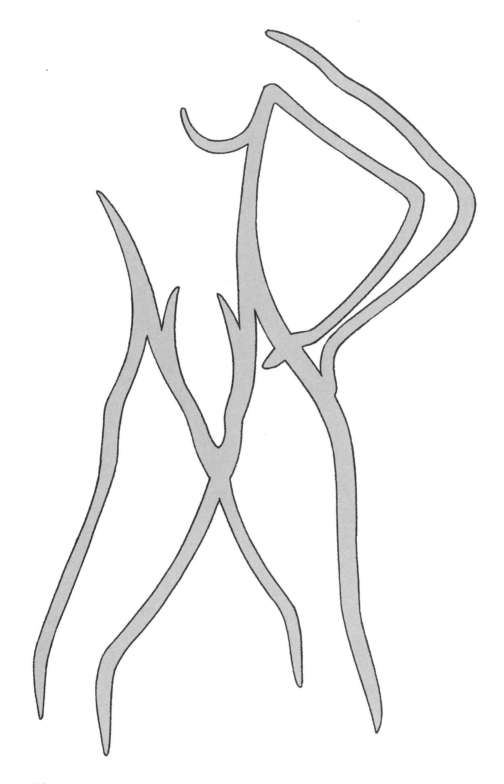

Woman.

Woman's head.

pping in pond. (See photo on page E of the color section.)

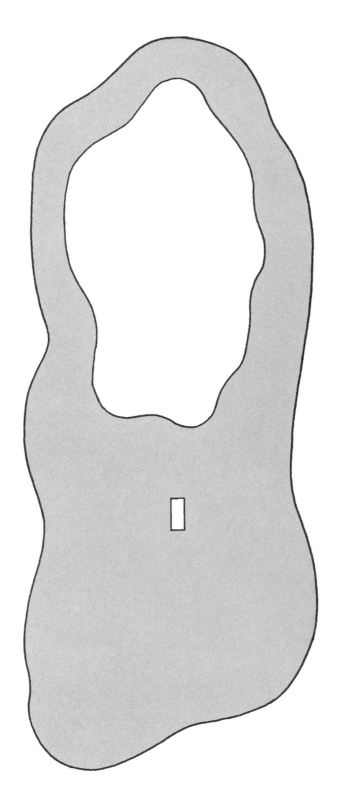

Base for woman stepping in pond.

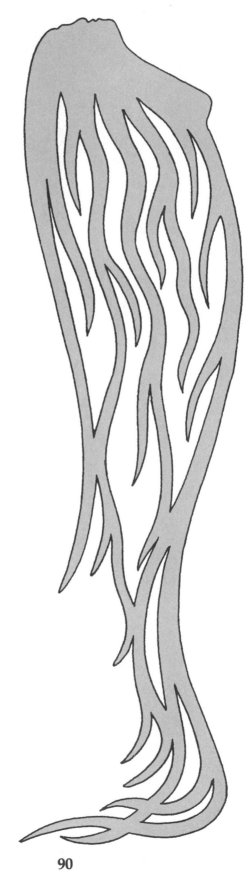

Woman with flowing hair. (See photo
on page E of the color section.)

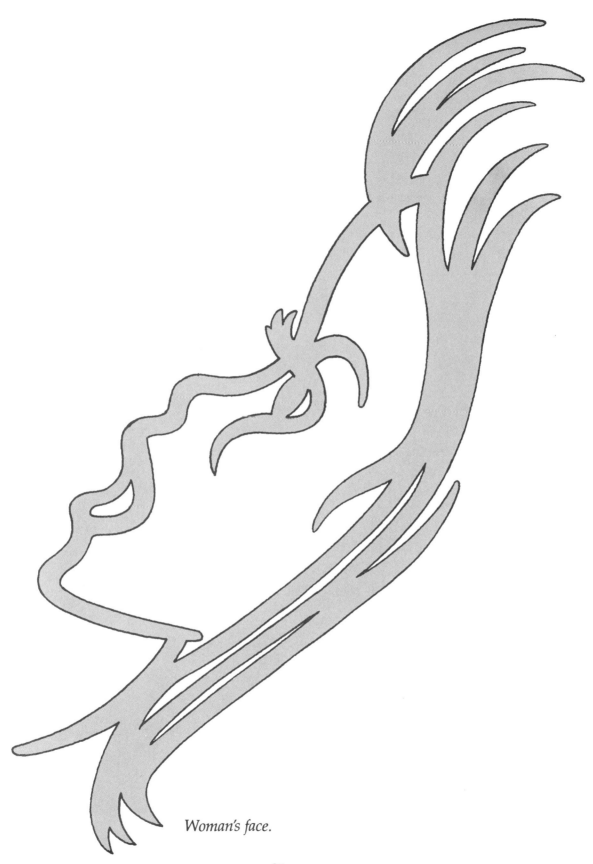

Woman's face.

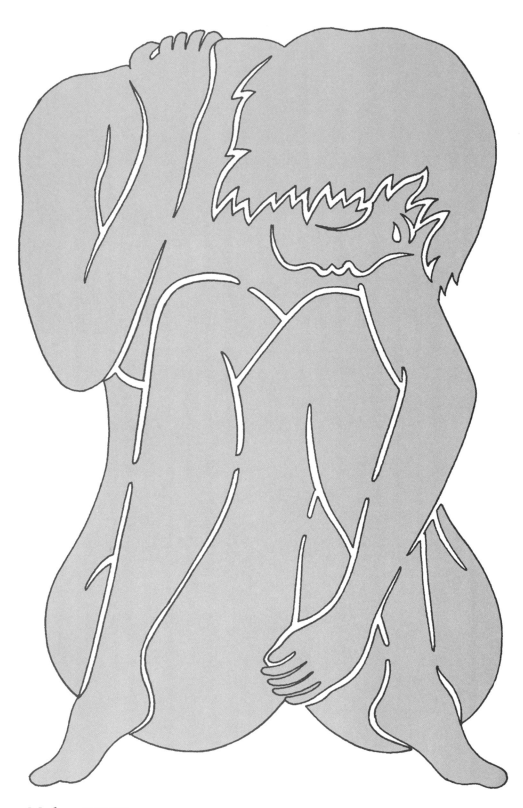

Modern woman.

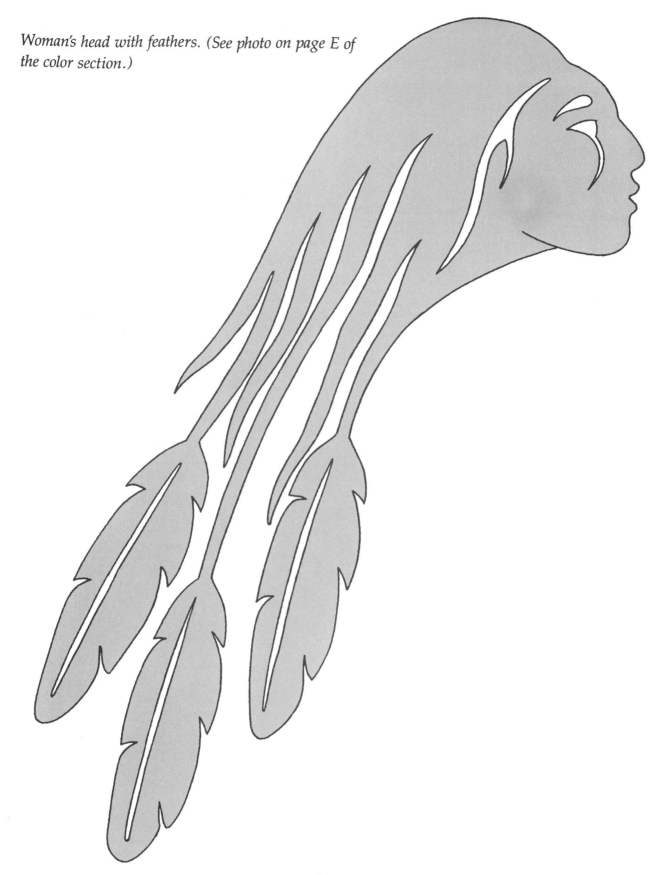

Woman's head with feathers. (See photo on page E of the color section.)

Woman and tree. This project is designed to be cut from three different-colored materials.

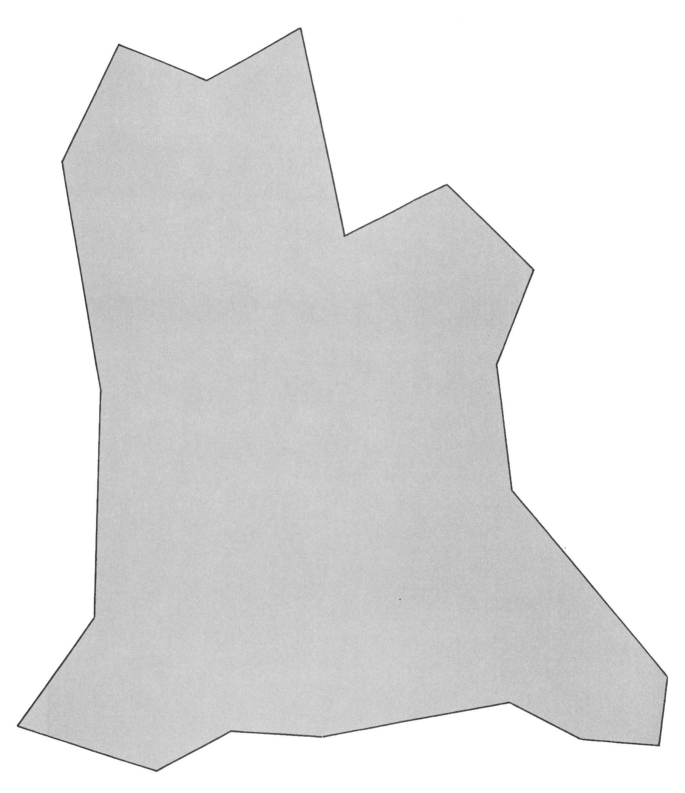

Plaque design for woman and tree.

Woman planting. The interior spaces could be filled with contrasting inlays.

MALE FORMS

Man's head. (See the photo on page E of the color section.)

Faces.

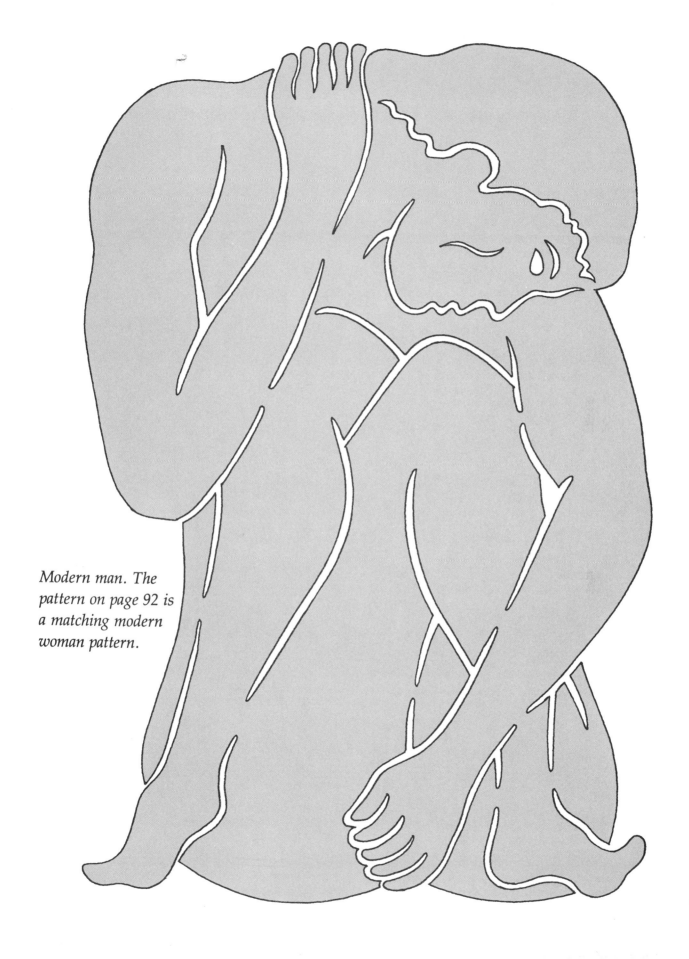

Modern man. The pattern on page 92 is a matching modern woman pattern.

Dancers

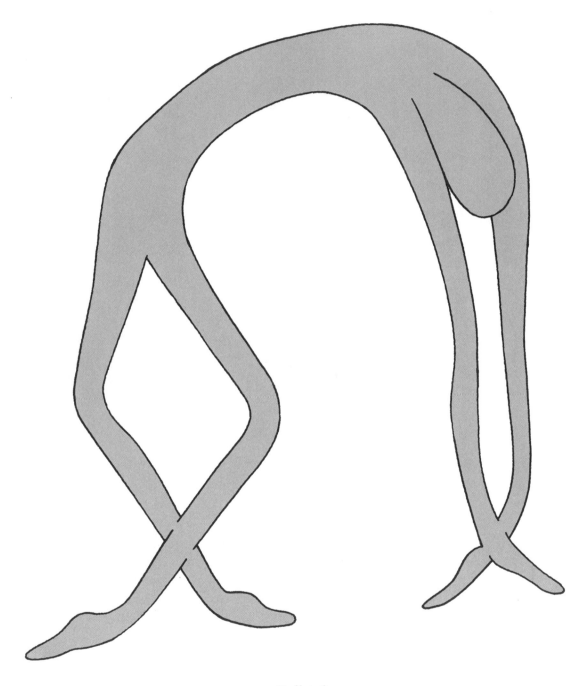

Ballet dancer.

Abstract dance.

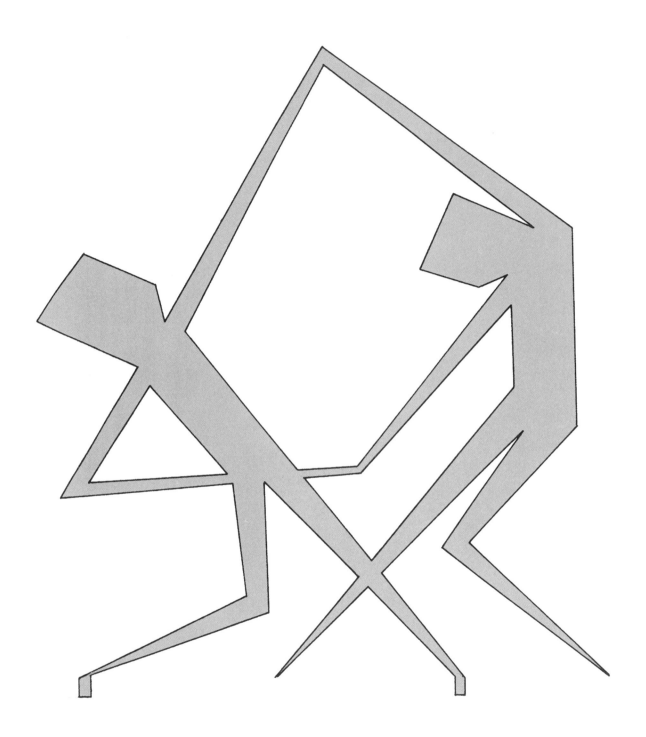

Last dance.

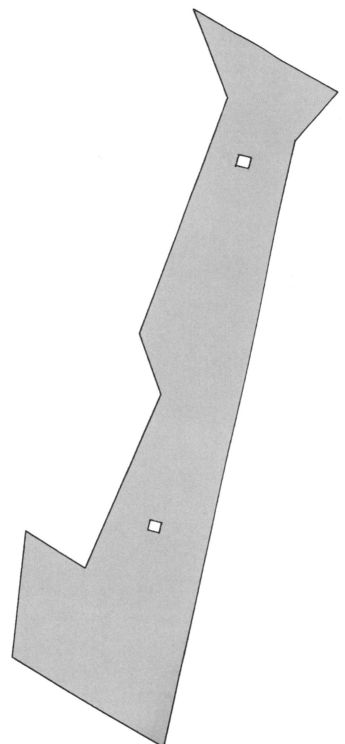

Base for last dance.

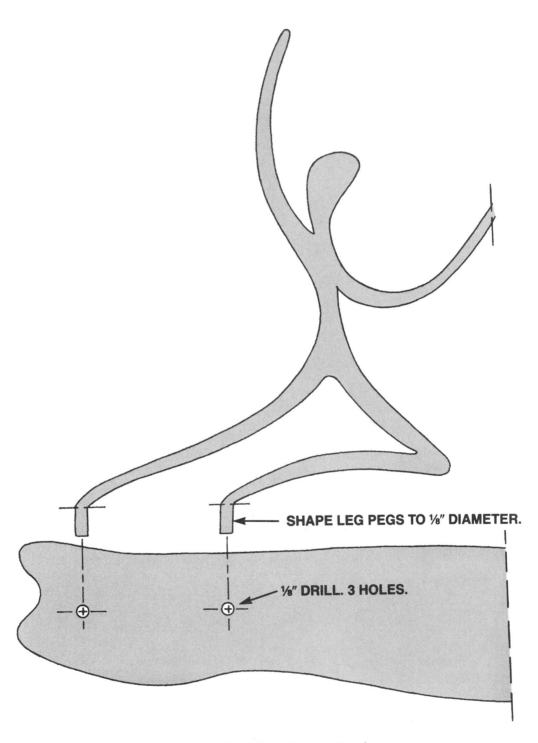

SHAPE LEG PEGS TO ⅛″ DIAMETER.

⅛″ DRILL. 3 HOLES.

Dancer. (See the photo on page F of the color section.)

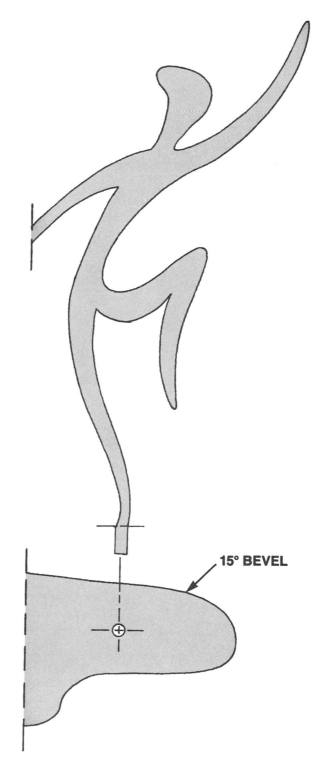

15° BEVEL

Continuation of dancer.

DRAGONS

Knight and dragon. (See the photo on page F of the color section.)

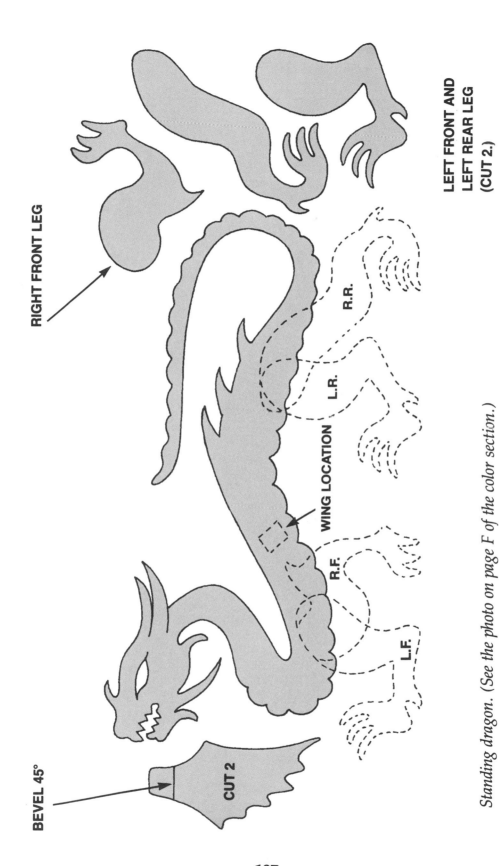

RIGHT FRONT LEG

LEFT FRONT AND
LEFT REAR LEG
(CUT 2.)

WING LOCATION

R.R.

L.R.

R.F.

L.F.

BEVEL 45°

CUT 2

Standing dragon. (See the photo on page F of the color section.)

Full-size upper leg detail for the dragon table. (See the photo on page F of the color section.)

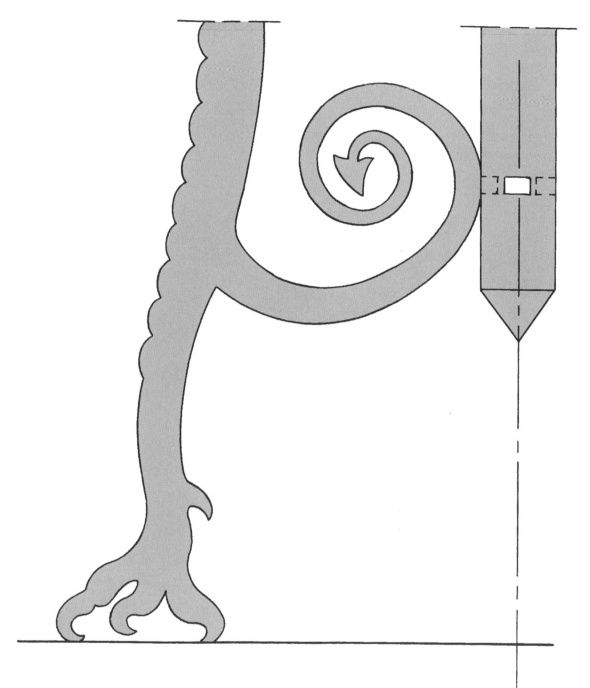

Full-size lower leg detail for the dragon table.

Top design for the dragon table. Enlarge the pattern 200%. Note: The dragon outline and rim of fire are saw-kerfed, piercing definition cuts.

EAGLES

Eagle.

Eagle. (See the photo on page G of the color section.)

FEATHERS

Eagle with feathers.

CUT 3 PIECES.

Eagle with feathers.

Eagle with feathers.

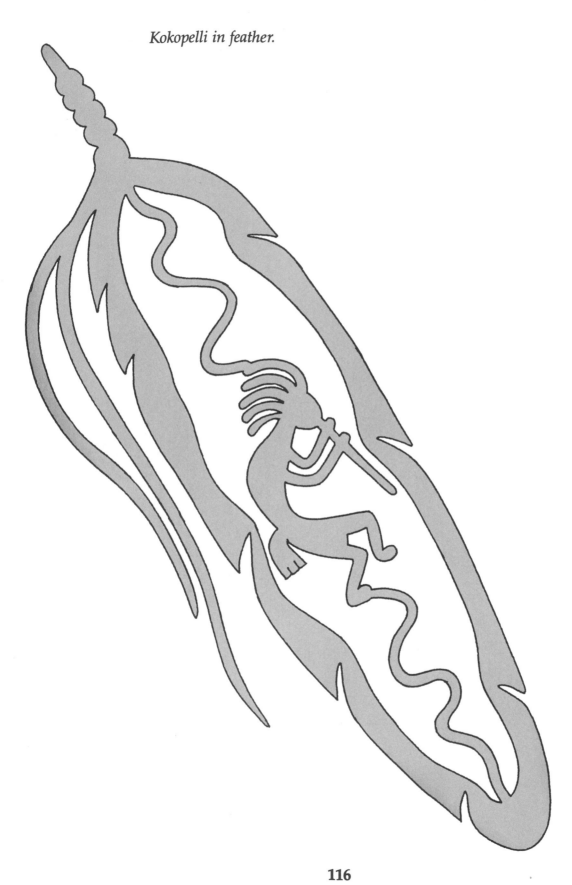

Kokopelli in feather.

Man in feather. (See the photo on page G of the color section.)

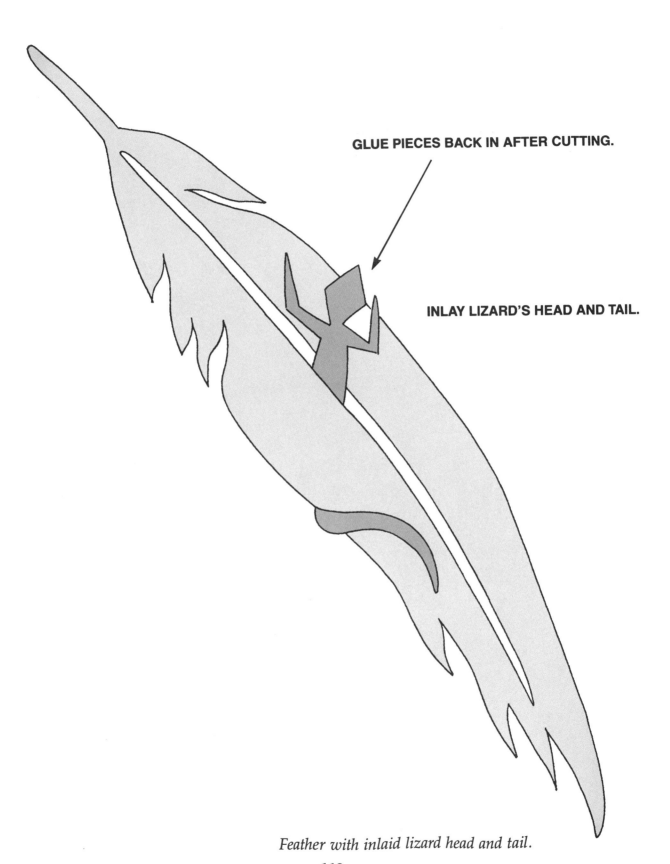

GLUE PIECES BACK IN AFTER CUTTING.

INLAY LIZARD'S HEAD AND TAIL.

Feather with inlaid lizard head and tail.

118

KOKOPELLIS

Kokopelli on moon.

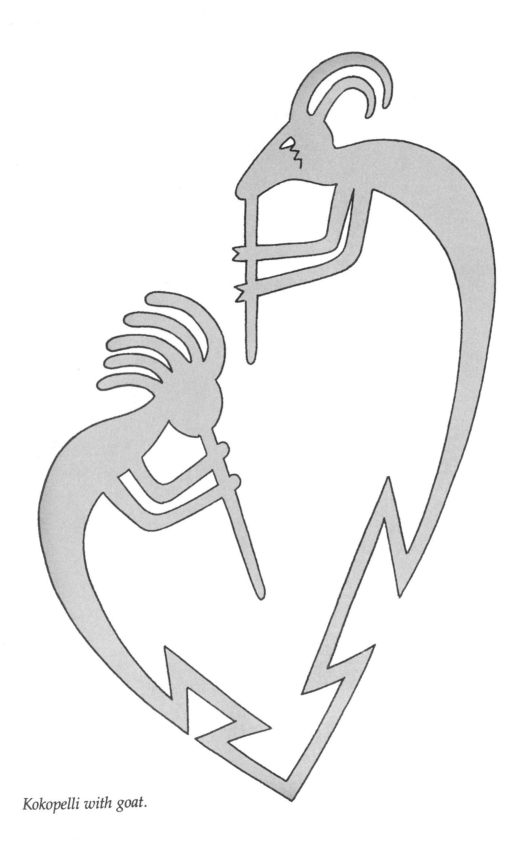

Kokopelli with goat.

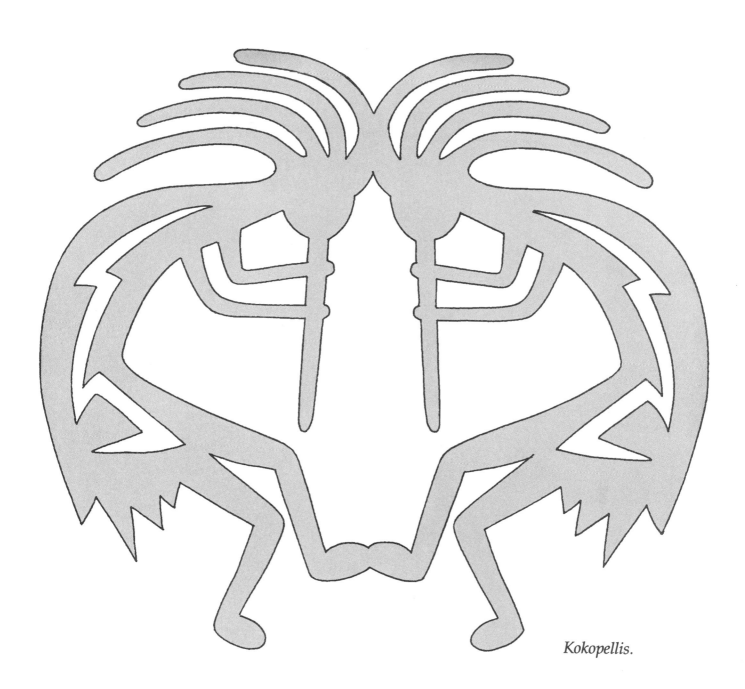

Kokopellis.

Kokopellis and feathers for metal or thin plywood.

FEATHERS. CUT 3.

122

SOUTHWEST DESIGNS

Eagle.

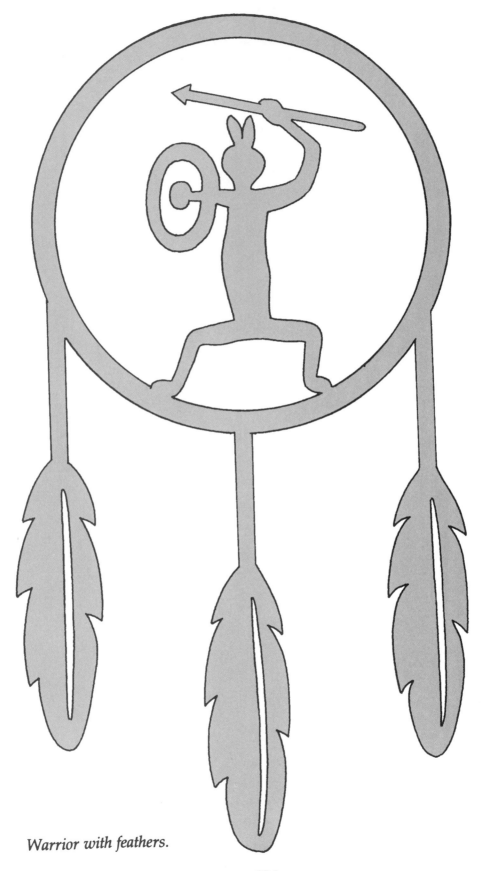

Warrior with feathers.

124

KOKOPELLI

GOAT

Alternate plywood or thin metal designs for inside-ring-with-feathers pattern on facing page. (See photo on page G of the color section.)

BEAR

SHAMAN

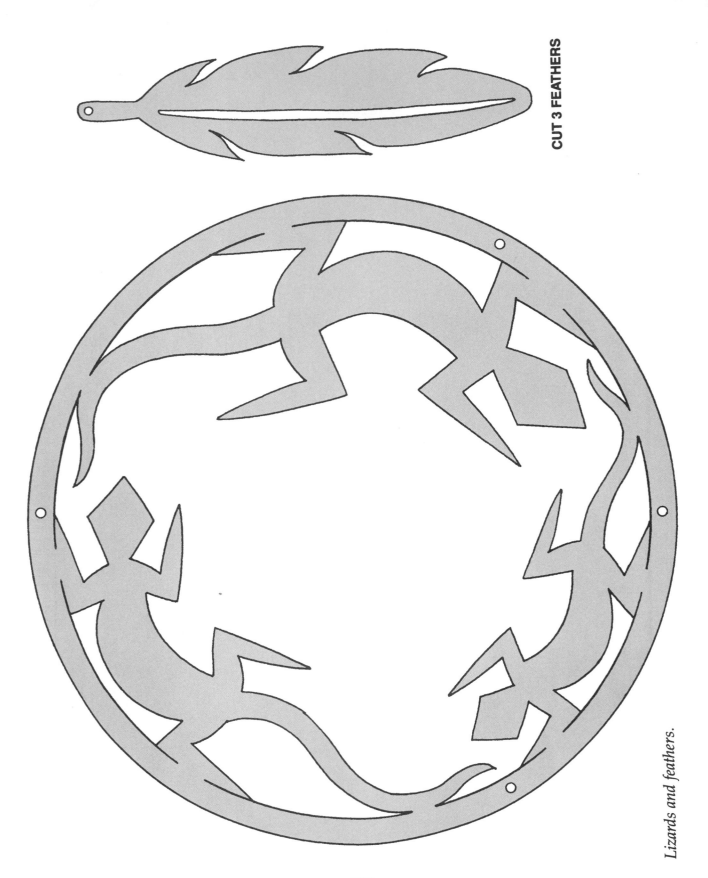

CUT 3 FEATHERS

Lizards and feathers.

126

Yei.

Rock men.

Rock man.

DESIGNS FOR METAL

Lizard and gecko metal patterns. Bend the legs as shown in photos on page H of the color section.

130

Earring and necklace designs. Inlays can be used in the inside internal spaces.

131

Tarantula and frog patterns for bent-metal projects. (See the photos on page H of the color section.)

Turtle and dragonfly patterns for bent-metal projects.

133

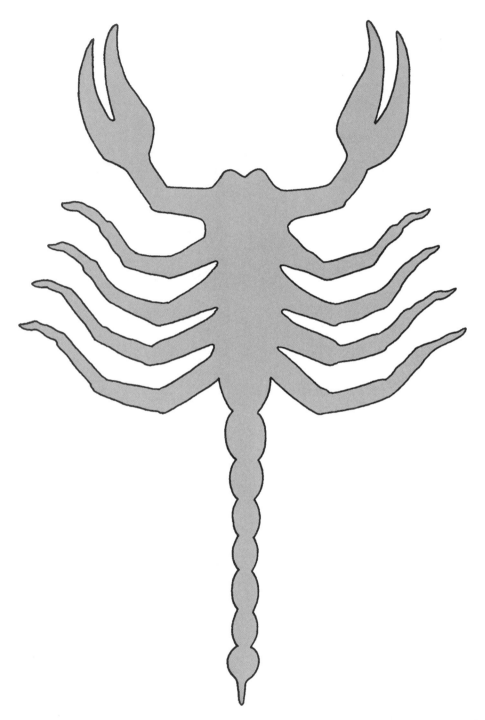

Scorpion pattern for bent-metal projects. (See the photos on page H of the color section.)

Praying mantis and horned toad patterns for bent-metal projects. (See the photo on page H of the color section.)

ABOUT THE AUTHORS

Patrick Spielman. Expert woodworker and innovator, brilliant teacher and best-selling author, Patrick Spielman has used his rare combination of talents to write over 50 of the most popular woodworking titles—including *The Router Handbook* (over 1,500,000 copies sold), *Scroll Saw Pattern Book*, *The Art of the Scroll Saw*, *The Art of the Lathe*, and numerous other pattern, project, tool, and technique books. As a master craftsman, he has also invented hundreds of jigs, fixtures, and other woodworking aids. He is a pioneer who has introduced scores of craftsmen to new and exciting avenues of woodworking, a technical consultant for tool manufacturers, and publisher of *Home Workshop News*—a color, bimonthly magazine dedicated to scroll sawing, router projects, and light woodworking activities. Patrick Spielman is one of the most respected authors in the field.

Dan Kihl. Co-author of the very successful book *Southwest Scroll Saw Patterns*, Dan Kihl has been making a living with a scroll saw for many years. Starting out in Wisconsin, where a friend gave him an old scroll saw, and needing products for his own gift shop, Dan com-

bined his artistic ability with a love of nature and began creating his own innovative designs.

Moving from Wisconsin to Arizona in 1989, Dan immediately became inspired by the area's natural beauty, wildlife, and Native American heritage. There he has developed several unique sculpturing processes utilizing the scroll saw and materials that capture the spirit of the Southwest. Recently, Dan has opened two art galleries in southern Arizona, one in the old mining town of Bisbee and the other in Tubac. Both locations feature his metal art sculptures and other works of art. Dan's metal sculptures are consistently on the leading edge of artistic creation and innovative technique.

From his vast library of designs, Dan has created several highly successful products that have been wholesaled to the gift industry all over the country. His unique style of scroll-saw patterns is highly praised and sought by professional scrollers all over the world. More of his scroll-saw designs can be found in the bimonthly publication *Home Workshop News*, to which Dan is also a regular contributor.

CURRENT BOOKS BY PATRICK SPIELMAN

THE ART OF THE LATHE: AWARD-WINNING DESIGNS

Enhance the decor of your home with twenty-seven stunning projects designed by master woodturners and presented in full color. These experts provide patterns, designs, instructions, and illustrations for creating a wide range of projects, which include elegant tree ornaments, spalted sycamore bowls, and exotic vases. 160 full-color pages.

THE ART OF THE SCROLL SAW: AWARD-WINNING DESIGNS

Wander through a spectacular, full-color gallery of extraordinary and imaginative scroll saw projects. Spielman is the tour guide through the exquisite exhibit of the work of 28 of the most widely known and productive woodworking artists in the United States and around the world. Follow their guidance and patterns and make an exciting assortment of 35 items, including doll furniture, a collapsible basket, a complete chess set, charming miniature clocks, a train puzzle, bookends, a picture frame, and much more. 160 full-color pages.

CHRISTMAS SCROLL SAW PATTERNS

Patrick and Patricia Spielman provide over 200 original, full-size scroll saw patterns with Christmas as the theme, including: toys; shelves; tree, window, and table decorations; segmented projects; and alphabets. A wide variety of Santas, trees, and holiday animals is included, as is a short, illustrated review of scroll-saw techniques. 4 pages in color. 164 pages.

CLASSIC FRETWORK SCROLL SAW PATTERNS

Spielman and co-author James Reidle provide over 140 imaginative patterns inspired by and derived from mid- to late-19th-century scroll-saw masters. This book covers nearly 30 categories of patterns and includes a brief review of scroll-saw techniques and how to work with patterns. The patterns include ornamental numbers and letters, beautiful birds, signs, wall pockets, silhouettes, a sleigh, jewelry boxes, toy furniture, and more. 192 pages.

COUNTRY MAILBOXES

Spielman and co-author Paul Meisel have come up with the 20 best country-style mailbox designs. They include an old pump fire wagon, a Western saddle, a Dalmatian, and even a boy fishing. Simple instructions cover cutting, painting, decorating, and installation. Over 200 illustrations. 4 pages in color. 164 pages.

GLUING & CLAMPING

A thorough, up-to-date examination of one of the most critical steps in woodworking. Spielman explores the features of every type of glue—from traditional animal-hide glues to the newest epoxies—the clamps and tools needed, the bonding properties of different wood species, safety tips, and all techniques from edge-to-edge and end-to-end gluing to applying plastic laminates. Also included is a glossary of terms. Over 500 illustrations. 256 pages.

MAKING COUNTRY-RUSTIC WOOD PROJECTS

Hundreds of photos, patterns, and detailed scaled drawings reveal construction methods, woodworking techniques, and Spielman's professional secrets for making indoor and outdoor furniture in the distinctly attractive Country-Rustic style. Covered are all aspects of furniture making from choosing the best wood for the job to texturing smooth boards. Among the dozens of projects are mailboxes, cabinets, shelves, coffee tables, weather vanes, doors, paneling, plant stands, and many other durable and economical pieces. 400 illustrations. 4 pages in color. 164 pages.

MAKING WOOD BOWLS WITH A ROUTER & SCROLL SAW

Using scroll-sawn rings, inlays, fretted edges, and much more, Spielman and master craftsman Carl Roehl have developed a completely new approach to creating decorative bowls. Over 200 illustrations. 8 pages in color. 168 pages.

MAKING WOOD DECOYS

This clear, step-by-step approach to the basics of decoy carving is abundantly illustrated with close-up photos for designing, selecting, and obtaining woods; tools; feather detailing; painting; and finishing of decorative and working decoys. Six different professional decoy artists are featured. Photo gallery (4 pages in full color) along with numerous detailed plans for various popular decoys. 164 pages.

MAKING WOOD SIGNS

Designing, selecting woods and tools, and every process through finishing are clearly covered. Instructions for hand- and power-carving, routing, and sandblasting techniques for small to huge signs. Foolproof guides for professional letters and ornaments. Hundreds of photos (4 pages in full color). Lists sources for supplies and special tooling. 148 pages.

New Router Handbook

This updated and expanded version of the definitive guide to routing continues to revolutionize router use. The text, with over 1,000 illustrations, covers familiar and new routers, bits, accessories, and tables available today; complete maintenance and safety techniques; a multitude of techniques for both hand-held and mounted routers; plus dozens of helpful shop-made fixtures and jigs. 384 pages.

Original Scroll-Saw Shelf Patterns

Patrick Spielman and Loren Raty provide over 50 original, full-size patterns for wall shelves, which may be copied and applied directly to wood. Photographs of finished shelves are included, as well as information on choosing woods, stack sawing, and finishing. 4 pages in color. 132 pages.

Realistic Decoys

Spielman and master carver Keith Bridenhagen reveal their successful techniques for carving, feather texturing, painting, and finishing wood decoys. Details you can't find elsewhere—anatomy, attitudes, markings, and the easy, step-by-step approach to perfect delicate procedures—make this book invaluable. Includes listings for contests and shows, and sources of tools and supplies. 274 close-up photos. 8 pages in color. 232 pages.

Router Basics

With over 200 close-up, step-by-step photos and drawings, this valuable starter handbook will guide the new owner, as well as provide a spark to owners for whom the router isn't the tool they turn to most often. Covers all the basic router styles, along with how-it-works descriptions of all its major features. Includes sections on bits and accessories, as well as square-cutting and trimming, case and furniture routing, cutting circles and arcs, template and freehand routing, and using the router with a router table. 128 pages.

Router Jigs & Techniques

A practical encyclopedia of information, covering the latest equipment to use with the router, it describes all the newest commercial routing machines, along with jigs, bits, and other aids and devices. The book not only provides invaluable tips on how to determine which router and bits to buy, it explains how to get the most out of the equipment once it is bought. Over 800 photos and illustrations. 384 pages.

Scroll Saw Basics

Features more than 275 illustrations covering basic techniques and accessories. Sections include types of saws, features, selection of blades, safety, and how to use patterns. Half a dozen patterns are included to help the scroll-saw user get started. Basic cutting techniques are covered, including inside cuts, bevel cuts, stack sawing, and others. 128 pages.

Scroll Saw Country Patterns

With 300 full-size patterns in 28 categories, this selection of projects covers an extraordinary range, with instructions every step of the way. Projects include farm animals, people, birds, and butterflies, plus letter and key holders, coasters, switch plates, country hearts, and more. Directions for piercing, drilling, sanding, and finishing, as well as tips on using special tools. 4 pages in color. 196 pages.

SCROLL SAW FRETWORK PATTERNS

This companion book to *Scroll Saw Fretwork Techniques & Projects* features over 200 fabulous, full-size fretwork patterns. These patterns, drawn by James Reidle, include popular classic designs, plus an array of imaginative contemporary ones. Choose from a variety of numbers, signs, brackets, animals, miniatures, silhouettes, and more. 256 pages.

SCROLL SAW HANDBOOK

The workshop manual to this versatile tool includes the basics (how scroll saws work, blades to use, etc.) and the advantages and disadvantages of the general types and specific brand-name models on the market. All cutting techniques are detailed, including compound and bevel sawing; making inlays, reliefs, and recesses; cutting metals and other non-woods; and marquetry. There's even a section on transferring patterns to wood. Over 500 illustrations. 256 pages.

SCROLL SAW HOLIDAY PATTERNS

Patrick and Patricia Spielman provide over 100 full-size, shaded patterns for easy cutting,

plus full-color photos of projects. Will serve all your holiday pleasures. Use these holiday patterns to create decorations, centerpieces, mailboxes, and diverse projects to keep or give as gifts. Standard holidays, as well as the four seasons, birthdays, and anniversaries, are represented. 8 pages of color. 168 pages.

SCROLL SAW PATTERN BOOK

The original classic pattern book—over 450 patterns for wall plaques, refrigerator magnets, candle holders, pegboards, jewelry, ornaments, shelves, brackets, picture frames, signboards, and many other projects. Beginning and experienced scroll saw users alike will find something to intrigue and challenge them. 256 pages.

SCROLL SAW PATTERNS FOR THE COUNTRY HOME

Patrick and Patricia Spielman and Sherri Spielman Valitchka produce a wide-ranging collection of over 200 patterns on country themes, including simple cutouts, mobiles, shelves, sculpture, pull toys, door and window toppers, clock holders, photo frames, layered pictures, and more. Over 80 black-and-white photos and 8 pages of color photos help you to visualize the steps involved as well as the finished projects. General instructions in Spielman's clear and concise style are included. 200 pages.

SCROLL SAW PUZZLE PATTERNS

Eighty full-size patterns for jigsaw puzzles, stand-up puzzles, and inlay puzzles. With meticulous attention to detail, Patrick and Patricia Spielman provide instructions and step-by-step photos, along with tips on tools and wood selection, for making dinosaurs, camels, hippopotami, alligators—even a family of elephants! Inlay puzzle patterns include basic shapes, numbers, an accurate piece-together map of the United States, and a host of other colorful educational and enjoyable games for children. 8 pages of color. 264 pages.

Scroll Saw Shelf Patterns

Spielman and master scroll saw designer Loren Raty offer full-size patterns for 44 different shelf styles. Designs include wall shelves, corner shelves, and multi-tiered shelves. The patterns work well with ¼-inch hardwood, plywood, or any solid wood. Over 150 illustrations. 4 pages in color. 132 pages.

Scroll Saw Silhouette Patterns

With over 120 designs, Spielman and James Reidle provide an extremely diverse collection of intricate silhouette patterns, ranging from Victorian themes to sports to cowboys. They also include mammals, birds, country and nautical designs, as well as dragons, cars, and Christmas themes. Tips, hints, and advice are included along with detailed photos of finished works. 160 pages.

Sharpening Basics

The ultimate handbook that goes well beyond the "basics" to become the major up-to-date reference work features more than 300 detailed illustrations (mostly photos), explaining every facet of tool sharpening. Sections include bench-sharpening tools, sharpening machines, and safety. Chapters cover cleaning tools, and sharpening all sorts of tools, including chisels, plane blades (irons), hand knives, carving tools, turning tools, drill and boring tools, router and shaper tools, jointer and planer knives, drivers and scrapers, and, of course, saws. 128 pages.

Southwest Scroll Saw Patterns

Spielman and scroll-sawing wizard Dan Kihl presents over 200 patterns inspired by the early cultures of the American Southwest. Designs include coyotes, buffalo, horses, lizards, snakes, pottery, cacti, cowboys, kokopelli figures, and more. Incorporate them into all kinds of projects: key racks, clocks, signs, shelves, napkin holders, jewelry boxes, and more. Follow the suggestions for using copper inlay on projects, either for a bright, shiny look or chemically aged to a beautiful bluish green for striking results that are not commonly seen in scroll-saw work. 8 pages of color. 168 pages.

Spielman's Original Scroll Saw Patterns

Over 250 full-size patterns that don't appear elsewhere feature teddy bears, dinosaurs, sports figures, dancers, cowboy cutouts, Christmas ornaments, and dozens more. Fretwork patterns are included for a Viking ship, framed cutouts, wall-hangers, key-chain miniatures, jewelry, and much more. Hundreds of step-by-step photos and drawings show how to turn, repeat, and crop each design for thousands of variations. 4 pages of color. 228 pages.

VICTORIAN GINGERBREAD: PATTERNS & TECHNIQUES

Authentic pattern designs (many full-size) cover the complete range of indoor and outdoor detailing: brackets, corbels, shelves, grilles, balusters, running trim, headers, valances, gable ornaments, pickets, trellises, and more. Also included are complete plans for Victorian mailboxes, house numbers, signs, and more. With clear instructions and helpful drawings by James Reidle, the book also provides tips for making gingerbread trim. 8 pages in color. 200 pages.

VICTORIAN SCROLL SAW PATTERNS

Intricate original designs plus classics from the 19th century are presented in full-size, shaded patterns. Instructions are provided with drawings and photos. Projects include alphabets and numbers, silhouettes and designs for shelves, frames, filigree baskets, plant holders, decorative boxes, picture frames, welcome signs, architectural ornaments, and much more. 160 pages.

WOODWORKER'S PATTERN LIBRARY: ALPHABETS & DESIGNS

Spielman and daughter Sherri Spielman Valitchka have come up with a collection of 40 alphabets and matching number patterns in the new series the *Woodworker's Pattern Library*. Upper- and lowercase alphabets are presented for all woodworking uses, including block script, italic, and a section on decorative design elements to complement uses of lettering. An introductory section on Basic Tips provides information on enlarging and transferring patterns as well as on making templates. 128 pages.

WOODWORKER'S PATTERN LIBRARY: BORDERS, TRIM & FRAMES

Spielman and designer Brian Dahlen continue the popular series with a collection of dozens of decorative patterns for scroll saw enthusiasts. Styles range from the basic with simple lines and little detail, to ornate swirls and curls and pictorial motifs. Create unusual name plates, house numbers, or clocks. Frame works of art, bulletin boards, and anything else that calls out for some pizzazz. Repetitive linear designs are included, and will work especially well in architectural applications around doors, windows, and archways. 128 pages.

WOODWORKER'S PATTERN LIBRARY: SPORTS FIGURES

Spielman and Brian Dahlen have put together a full range of sports-related patterns for the new series the *Woodworker's Pattern Library*. Sports images for scroll-sawing enthusiasts include over 125 patterns in 34 categories of sporting activity. The patterns can be incorporated in functional projects such as signs or furniture and shelves, or they can be used simply for decorative accent such as silhouettes in windows or against walls. 128 pages.

ACKNOWLEDGMENTS

The authors express their sincere thanks and appreciation for the helpful efforts with this work from the following individuals: Brandon Kihl and Victoria Ramos for their special design assistance; Dirk Boelman for his skilled ink tracings of our drawings; and Julie Kiehnau for her expert scroll-cut sample projects and typing.

INDEX

Pages in bold refer to color section.